THE ART OF THE
TEA TOWEL

THE ART OF THE
TEA TOWEL

OVER 100 OF THE BEST DESIGNS

Marnie Fogg

BATSFORD

DEDICATION

In memory of Ruth Wass Wright

First published in the United Kingdom in 2018 by Batsford
43 Great Ormond Street
London WC1N 3HZ
An imprint of Pavilion Books Company Ltd

ISBN: 9781849945028

A CIP catalogue record for this book is available
from the British Library.

25 24 23 22 21 20 19 18
10 9 8 7 6 5 4 3 2 1

Reproduction by Mission Productions, Hong Kong
Printed by Toppan Leefung Printing Ltd, China

This book can be ordered direct from the publisher at the website
www.pavilionbooks.com, or try your local bookshop.

Distributed in the United States and Canada by
Sterling Publishing Co., Inc. 1166 Avenue of the Americas,
17th Floor, New York, NY 10036

CONTENTS

INTRODUCTION

'The trusty tea towel is good – not the
grubby rag that has been hanging on the
door for a week but a crisply linen one.
I love tea towels. I love having a constantly
high pile of them in the cupboard and
I really like them to be pressed.'

RITA KONIG, INTERIOR DESIGNER AND JOURNALIST

ANY ELEVATION of the humble tea towel to the status of cultural icon may seem a bold assertion; but as a metaphor conveying totemic aspects of domesticity, stability and design creativity it has attracted nuanced contexts that deserve reflection and a level of celebration.

Since its emergence as a manufactured artefact during the Industrial Revolution of the 19th century, the mass-produced tea towel has provided a microcosm of domestic iconography – far exceeding the confines of its very obvious utility. It has become an essential memento of leisure spending, purchased from museums, country-house properties and holidays, as well as commemorating significant national events – a royal wedding or jubilee, encouraging an entire community to share the experience.

Most significantly, tea towels have operated as vehicles for a host of design movements, acting as a medium supporting all the characteristics of a broader graphic style, from the artwork of designers such as Lucienne Day to that of Pat Albeck, renowned for her work for the National Trust.

This book charts the evolution of the tea towel from the linen cloth – frequently embroidered in the 18th century to match the table linen and initially used to keep the teapot warm – to an essential styling accessory for contemporary kitchens, produced by practitioners as diverse as iconoclastic fashion designer Matty Bovan and printmaker Angela Harding. It is a form of democratic art, a vehicle for artists and printmakers to disseminate their work to a wider audience, outside the curated work of a gallery. The tea towel may also offer a disruptive comment on society, matching the poster and T-shirt as an effective and powerful form of sloganeering.

The canvas was initially linen, a natural fibre or fabric made from the cultivated flax plant, *Linum usitatissimum*. Prized for its softness and stronger when wet than dry, it has a smooth surface, making the final fabric lint-free. Early 20th-century household manuals occasionally called them glass towels. Progress in manufacturing textiles has changed the materials used to make tea towels to less expensive fibres, particularly cotton, or a mix of linen and cotton called Linen Union. The Linen Union tea towel is a 55 per cent linen, 45 per cent cotton mix, bleached white. It offers a more open weave and is popular within the heritage market. Sizes are generally uniform, 78 x 48cm (30¾ x 19in), creating a print area of 72 x 42cm (28¼ x 16½in). During the latter part of the 1990s, advances in digital printing and dye development – where an image can be sent directly from a computer to the cloth – became an option to replace the labour-intensive process of conventional silk-screen printing, where the cost of short runs is prohibitive due to the inevitable investment in colour separations, screen preparation and production downtime. The new technology allows the freelance designer and producer to experiment without too much initial outlay and also enables the ready exploitation and manufacture of heritage and archival subject matter from vintage posters and so on, such as those sold at Heal's.

By the 19th century and the early to mid-20th century, a glass towel or tea towel would most likely have been a striped or checked cloth. The first commercially successful printed tea towels were pioneered by Swedish-born designer Astrid Sampe in 1955. Trained at the Swedish University of Arts, Crafts and Design (Konstfack) in Stockholm, and later at the Royal College of Art in London, in 1937 she started working as a designer at Nordiska Kompaniet, and a year later became the manager of the newly created NK Textile Studio (Textilkammaren). She revolutionized the traditional use of linen with the collection Linnelinjen ('Linen Line'), a range of textiles that included tea towels, launched at the Helsingborg Exhibition in 1955. The most influential of these was inspired by Astrid Sampe's *Persson's Spice Rack*, dedicated to the ceramist Signe Persson Melin, who, in the early 1950s, made a series of ceramic spice jars with cork heads. The design continues to remain a bestseller. Astrid's personal ethos, 'Order is Freedom', is reflected in the graphic symmetry and straight lines of her aesthetic and set the template for the designs which were to follow: versions of various kitchen paraphernalia, storage jars, utensils, and items of food such as fish and fruit. Shortly afterwards, Lucienne Day was commissioned by the Irish linen company Thomas Somerset & Co. of Belfast and their subsidiary Fragonard Ltd to revitalize a flagging Irish linen business, resulting in a series of groundbreaking and commercially successful designs that secured the place of the tea towel firmly at the high end of design.

The highly decorative printed tea towel flourished during the 1950s and '60s – a period during which printed textiles burgeoned following the era of wartime austerity. This was kick-started by the Festival of Britain in 1951, and flourished during the following decade when print, illustration and graphics were a pervasive presence in modern life. During periods when minimalism was the prevailing aesthetic, the tea towel was chosen for its utility, more often a plain cloth with jacquard text proclaiming 'glass cloth', woven into a blue or red stripe, or the traditional checked waffle weave. However, there is now a new interest in the artistic and commercial potential of the printed tea towel, evidenced by the involvement of designers, artists and printmakers in the genre.

THE 1950S

'It takes a woman to think up
a design idea that other women
have been wanting for years.'

LUCIENNE DAY, TEXTILE DESIGNER

For the beauty of it...
for the life of it...

Lay linoleum for its colour gaiety and hygienic cleanliness —for the atmosphere of 'perpetual spring' it brings to every room during a long life of hard wear.

"FANDANGO" DESIGN C683

LAY WILLIAMSON LINOLEUM

LINOLEUM is quiet to the tread

LINOLEUM is resilient

LINOLEUM is easy to clean

LINOLEUM resists abrasion

LINOLEUM for long life

Here's a new suggestion for a colourful floor in Linoleum. It is a design called "FANDANGO" and comes from a wide range of linoleums produced by Jas. Williamson & Son Ltd., Lancaster, long renowned for the quality and reliability of their products. Modernize and brighten your Kitchen-Dinette by using the new "Fandango" design as illustrated. You will find this and many other distinctive patterns by Williamson at stores throughout the country.

LINOLEUM

JAS. WILLIAMSON & SON LTD., LANCASTER. BARRY, OSTLERE & SHEPHERD LTD., DUNDEE LINOLEUM CO. LTD., LINOLEUM MANUFACTURING CO. LTD.
MICHAEL NAIRN & CO. LTD., NORTH BRITISH LINOLEUM CO. LTD., SCOTTISH CO-OPE...

ELMA

FOLLOWING the bleak austerity of World War II, engineering brilliance and creative energy once deployed for wartime necessities became focused on domestic design. Colour and pattern were introduced to household goods as innovations in interior product design flourished. Consigned once more to the domestic sphere after the relative freedom enjoyed during the exigencies of war work, women elevated the kitchen beyond a place of simple utility, for some previously the domain of servants, to become the heart of the home. Here, the housewife directed her energies to incorporating style and novelty into the epicentre of her domestic empire. The evolving domestic aesthetic incorporated a feminine version of Modernism, and expendable ephemera such as small kitchen accessories in the form of tableware and tea towels allowed her a freedom of expression that was otherwise lacking in the narrowly prescribed life of the 1950s housewife. Under her dominion, the kitchen became a social space and an arena for display, with the division of labour sharply defined between the sexes.

New scientific materials usurped the role of traditional surface finishes. Seats were glossily vinyl covered, while tables and cupboard fronts were transformed with plastic laminates, such as Con-Tact, a sticky-backed vinyl film developed in 1954, or the more durable Formica – each flaunting brighter colours and washable, stain-resistant surfaces. These allowed an overall scheme of colour and pattern in which the tea towel played an integral part. Stylization and abstraction infused the prevailing aesthetic. The result was an inflection of both scientific modernity and the high culture of international modern art, with forms vaunted by sculptors like Gabo, Hepworth, Arp and Picasso subliminally influencing the domestic landscape. Pattern took on dynamic asymmetrical forms, such as the pointed boomerang, a symbol of movement and flight, or the artist's palette with its blobs of vibrant colour. Scientific advances provided the molecule as inspiration, as did skeletal plant forms and the work of artists that included Alexander Calder and Joan Miró.

These influences came to fruition in both textiles and ceramics, such as Terence Conran's *Chequers*. This was developed in 1957, based on a design Conran originally created in 1951 for the textile manufacturer David Whitehead. Enid Seeney's *Homemaker* tableware for Ridgway Potteries, designed in 1955, was decorated with everyday contemporary items. Seeney incorporated a representation of a chair designed by Robin Day, exemplifying the cross-fertilization and integration of design ideas across a broad spectrum of products. When the Institute of Contemporary Art (ICA) was founded in 1947 it emblemized the new panorama of post-war optimism and creativity in the single word 'contemporary', bridging all sectors – including art, architecture, product, graphic design and textiles. In this period textile design pioneers were legion, including Marian Mahler, Tom Mellor, Jacqueline Groag and Lucienne Day, who produced several designs for the influential Festival of Britain in 1951. This exhibition was staged to promote the most exciting and progressive in new British design. Day's influential *Calyx* design retailed through Heal's Fabrics and resulted in a plethora of copies. Technical developments, for example the use of of automatic screen printing, reduced the cost and fuelled the introduction of new patterns to the marketplace, enabling these designs to be accessible to a wider audience.

Although wartime food rationing continued until 1954, representations of utopian domesticity and fanciful consumption – from flowering geraniums in terracotta plant pots or trailing ivy over a trellis, to fruit in bowls, wine glasses, jugs, vases and kitchen utensils – all featured on the contemporary tea towel. In this way daily minutiae were to be seen as a celebration and resurrection of the importance of the home and the stability of family households.

"TOO MANY COOKS" A FRAGONARD DESIGN BY LUCIENNE DAY IRISH LINEN FAST COLOURS

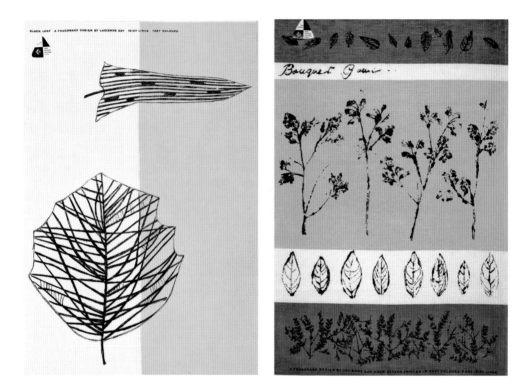

Left: At the risk of spoiling the broth, Lucienne Day designed *Too Many Cooks* in 1959 for Thomas Somerset's Fragonard range. It gained a Design Centre Award in 1960 and was a popular commercial product, offered in a variety of colourways.

Above left: One of three designs from 1959 by Lucienne Day for Fragonard that gained a Design Centre Award, *Black Leaf* is a very spare, two colour, two screen figurative composition that comes close to pure abstraction.

Above right: On and between bold bands of warm tones, Lucienne Day superimposes and interlays informal natural images in black, in the form of hand script and physical offprints from herbs. *Bouquet Garni* for Fragonard won both a Design Centre Award and a Gold Medal at the California State Fair in 1960.

Above: *Trooping the Colour* from Ulster Weavers is a study in obtaining optimum 'realism' from a finite number of screens. Each of the separated colours is distributed into as many figurative components as is viable for legibility. Overprint tones are also exploited to imply a wider colour gamut, although the effect remains graphically naïve.

Right: Quartered to do justice to four emblematic national edifices – St. Paul's Cathedral, Westminster Abbey, Buckingham Palace and the Tower of London – this pure linen memento of the 1953 Coronation enlists a cornucopia of elemental regalia to celebrate the occasion. The crown of St. Edward and the Gold State Coach are elegantly rendered in the midst of garlanded swags of ribbon, flags and regal flora.

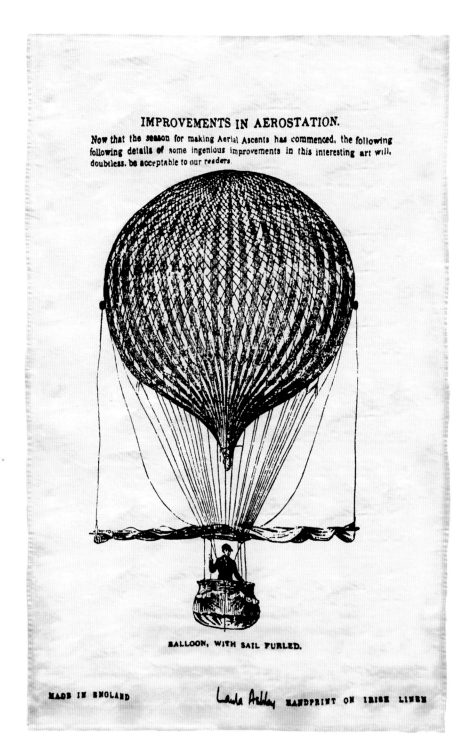

The Laura Ashley company was founded in 1953, with Laura Ashley and her husband Bernard printing by the silk screen process in their London flat. The image is lifted from the Victorian ballad monger and pamphleteer, James Catnatch of Seven Dials, London.

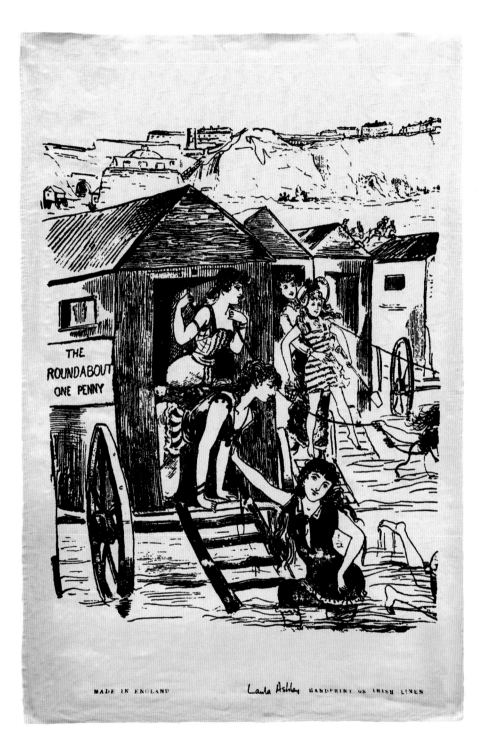

One of a series of Laura Ashley tea towels based on Victorian advertisements and playbills that recall with mild irony the nostalgic pleasures of simpler times. The single-colour images are silk screened directly onto the cloth by hand.

SONG OF THE STEAM COACHMAN *THAT* DRIVES THE OMNIBUS TO THE MOON.

Steam carriages by land are now the order of the day, sir,
But why they haven't started yet, 'tis not for me to say, sir ;
Some people hint 'tis *uphill* work—that loose they find a screw, sir,
Such novelties, as Pat would say, of *old* they never *knew*, sir.

Now is the time for a sly trip to *the Moon*, sir,

There's a new RAIL ROAD just made through *the Sky*,

Or if you prefer it, we have a *prime* BALLOON, sir,

In which you can ascend with me *up sky high*.

Travelling the rage is—in the tying of a sandal,

We take our *tea* in *Tartary*, or *chop* at *Coromandel*,

Then when *blazing hot* we get with *India's gums* and *spices*,

We take a *stroll* towards the *Pole*, and *cool our-selves with ices*,

Now is the time for a sly trip to *the Moon*, sir, &c.

CRAMPTON'S PATENT EXPRESS ENGINE 1851

MADE IN WALES   *Laura Ashley* HANDPRINT   LINEN

Left: James Catnatch, a London printer, conducted his trade in chapbooks and broadside ballads over several decades, working until his death in 1841 with woodcut artists such as Thomas Bewick. Laura Ashley found his publications a rich source for her early tea-towel prints.

Above: Thomas Crampton exhibited his patented 'Liverpool' Express Steam Engine in the 1851 Great Exhibition to extensive international acclaim, becoming the byword for express travel across Europe. This engraving from his patent application adorns an early Laura Ashley tea towel.

SWALLOWTAIL BUTTERFLY
Papilio machaon britannicus

IRISH LINEN   BUTTERFLY SWALLOWTAIL BY ULSTER   Reg No 7926   MADE IN IRELAND

Both old and new world swallowtails are habitual denizens of wild carrot,
visiting through all stages of their metamorphosis. Here Ulster Weavers
illuminates this butterfly with the precision of a lepidoptery guide.

THE ROYAL SOCIETY FOR THE PROTECTION OF BIRDS   PURE IRISH LINE

Based in Norfolk, Robert Gillmor is a founder member and former president of the
Society of Wildlife Artists. The RSPB commissioned this species compendium of
over-wintering British birds.

PURE IRISH LINEN

ORIGINAL DESIGN BY DOROTHY MILLER

During the 1950s idiosyncratic subject matter and whimsical imagery presaged the use of popular culture as art form later seen in the work of the 1960s Pop Artists. This doe-eyed transgression in donkey form by Dorothy Miller caters for the Costa package sub-culture.

The poodle had a particular place in 1950s iconography, representing European 'sophistication'. However, Dorothy Miller introduces kitsch into the kitchen with a poodle puppy adorned in ribbon bows sitting in a chrysanthemum pot.

THE 1960s

'Since teacloths are a fairly cheap and
expendable product, the design of them
can be experimental. When paying a
small amount of money for something
that is not going to have a very long life,
people are prepared to take a risk and
buy exciting designs.'

PAT ALBECK, TEXTILE DESIGNER

ALTHOUGH contemporary style remained a continuing influence throughout the early 1960s, by 1964 the look of the post-war period segued into a fresher, more vibrant aesthetic, spearheaded by a coterie of youthful designers. The emergence of pop culture and the youth revolution led to the elevation of colour and pattern over form, and large-scale single motifs and geometric, flat, stylized florals appeared alongside the visual distortions of the Op-Art inspired patterns of artists such Bridget Riley and Victor Vasarely. Reproductions of the red, white and blue Union flag appeared alongside target and bull's eye motifs utilized by the Pop Art movement, which assembled cultural icons and found objects and transformed them into high art.

Full employment led to a consumer revolution and the young middle classes aspired to a different kind of kitchen than that of their parents. Couples setting up home had an awareness of modern design. Women, in the main back in the workplace, at least until children were born, now rejected the boredom of the mechanized kitchen and expected to share domestic duties with their husband. Cooking, shared by both partners, became a significant leisure pursuit prompted in part by the influential food writer Elizabeth David, who opened a shop selling imported kitchen equipment in London in 1965.

Shopping became a destination experience with the blossoming of fashion boutiques, such as trend-setting Mary Quant's Bazaar and the opening of Terence Conran's Habitat in 1964. The designer and entrepreneur was on a mission to reform domestic design in Britain, and the store featured simple and unpretentious artefacts like unglazed pots, wicker baskets, simple batterie de cuisine and the chicken brick. Habitat's interiors with their whitewashed brick walls, quarry tiles, spotlights, stripped pine and open shelving units were to become highly influential. The catalogue, introduced in 1966 and designed by Juliet Glynn-Smith, who also designed textiles including tea towels for the company, made these products accessible to those living outside London. Tea towels began to be produced with matching products, including oven gloves, aprons, table napkins, enamelled tin trays and cast-iron casserole dishes, to provide a cohesive look.

Heal Fabrics, introduced in the 1940s as an offshoot of the furniture and furnishings store Heal & Son, was at the forefront of textile design innovation. Led by Tom Worthington, the firm's managing director from 1948–71, the company averaged 30 new designs a year. Worthington built up relationships with young designers such as Barbara Brown, a graduate of London's Royal College of Art and Heal's most high-profile designer. Her adoption of large-scale precise geometric forms and undisguised repetition was in contrast to the more free-flowing aesthetic of Jyoti Bhomik. Born in India, Bhomik designed exclusively for Heal's in the 1960s, purveying an aesthetic inspired by the colours and patterns found in the Indian sub-continent. Towards the end of the decade, print design evoked images purloined from other cultures, fuelled by the popularity of the 'hippie trail' to India, Morocco and the Far East.

Heal's main rival for experimental design was Hull Traders, whose fabrics were marketed under the brand name Time Present. Under the auspices of design and colour consultant Shirley Craven, the fabrics were hand screen-printed using mainly pigment dyes – which float on the surface of the cloth unlike vat dyes that penetrate the cloth – allowing the company to produce short runs of experimental designs. Shirley Craven became a director of the company in 1963 in addition to her role as chief designer.

Designer Pat Albeck worked for the John Lewis Partnership, under its own brand name, Jonelle, which was launched in 1937. Albeck, an alumnus of the Royal College of Art, produced work in her freelance portfolio for a diverse range of clients including the National Trust, Sekers, Marks & Spencer and Sanderson. During this period, she was asked by John Lewis to produce a design based on the patterns of William Morris – her response was *Daisy Chain* – printed in several colourways. This became its best seller for 15 years, and in 2014 was reworked to celebrate the 150th anniversary of the store.

The Modernism of the early 1960s was discarded with the counter-revolution of 1968 when historical revivalism resulted in an eclectic appropriation of the past. Changes in trends accelerated as the decade progressed, although flat florals continued to have a popular appeal as a diffused domestic engagement with flower power.

The 1960s heralded a golden age of poster art. It defined the aesthetic of the counter-culture revolution and represented a youth culture undergoing psychedelic enlightenment with the use of LSD, a hallucinogenic drug that introduced pharmacological turmoil to the visual arts. The burgeoning hippie movement eagerly embraced this new psychedelic graphic style, which resulted in kaleidoscopic patterns, distorted fonts and heightened vibrant colours, all of which contributed to the broad visual language of the period. This distinctive style was necessarily diffused and domesticated by the contemporary kitchen textile market, one of the leading exponents of the genre being designer Ian Logan. Together with a group of textile design students from the Central School of Art and Design (now Central St Martins) Logan formed a small fabric print company called JRM Design, producing prints for fashion designers Mary Quant and Jeff Banks. The company also produced designs on cushions, tablecloths and tea towels.

Good Food was designed by Lucienne Day for Fragonard in 1961–2. Effected with linocut simplicity, this tea towel depicts an eclectic range of culinary constituents from oysters to the humble tomato.

By the hand of Lucienne Day for Fragonard, a simple colour tiled chequerboard readily suggests a backdrop for the food of a Provençal kitchen – tapenade, pistou, ratatouille and fresh figs.

Night and Day   designed by Lucienne Day®   twentytwentyone   made in Ireland

Lucienne Day exploits the release from repeat-pattern obligations to compose a canvas
of yin and yang graphic simplicity, wittily defining the temporal dichotomy of sun and moon.
Made in Ireland using 100% linen, the design was originally launched in 1962.

Batterie de Cuisine   designed by Lucienne Day®   twentytwentyone

Batterie de Cuisine

made in Ireland

Ron Crawford, a director of Belfast firm Nova Products, originally commissioned *Batterie de Cuisine* in the 1960s. The language and kitchenalia chosen by Day set this glass cloth firmly in the idiom of adherents of food writer Elizabeth David.

Diabolo is a Lucienne Day design from 1962. The opposed delta colour motif is fragmented by additional geometric fields of angular textures, creating depth and visual dynamism, akin to the abstract patterning of Paul Klee.

TUDOR TABLE   A **bestlinen** DESIGN BY LUCIENNE DAY   FAST COLOURS ON PURE LINEN MADE IN IRELAND

Ancient regal banquet prerogatives of garnished swan, pond carp and disembodied wild boar are asserted in Lucienne Day's *Tudor Table* design for bestlinen brand. The paper stencil approach gives a cartoonish simplicity to the reversed-out animal forms.

PERIWINKLE   A bestlinen DESIGN BY LUCIENNE DAY   FAST COLOURS ON PURE LINEN MADE IN IRELAND

Well-behaved *Vinca major* tendrils are held to attention astride a regimented colour stripe. In 1964 Lucienne Day created *Periwinkle* in three bold screen separations for bestlinen brand.

Lucienne Day populates her pattern-striped frieze with animated and light-hearted visual playfulness and a potpourri of typefaces in her bestlinen brand design, *Many Hands Make Light Work*, of 1964.

ROSE DIAMOND   A LUCIENNE DAY DESIGN IN PURE IRISH LINEN

NOVA
PRODUCTS

Making graphic reference to the phenomenon of crystalline defraction, as harnessed by skilled diamond cutters, Lucienne Day creates a spectral illusion of faceted depth in her *Rose Diamond* design of 1969 for Nova Products.

Tudor Garden by Lucienne Day casts a bird's eye view over a formal parterre. Banded in box to segregate lupin from lily, the strict geometry and horticultural palette amount to a striking graphic in this design for Nova Products.

100% COTTON   MADE IN U.K.

Left: From genesis in 1965 to final demise in 1977, the boutique brand, I was Lord Kitchener's Valet, provided a shorthand for all things retail inherent in the Swinging Sixties of London. In this diffusion merchandise item from its latter-day decline, the brand satirises its own psychedelic heritage of ironic subversion of historic military costume in tandem with noting the clichéd tourist location off Regent Street.

Above: In 1965 Pete Townsend of The Who donned the Union Flag in jacket form to go with the 1966 launch of their single, 'The Kids are Alright'. An expression of subversive Op-Art sensitivity rather than a jingoistic salute to queen and country, the fragmented red, white and blue graphic has had numerous reincarnations in popular culture.

IRISH LINEN   BY ULSTER REG No 7114   MADE IN IRELAND

"Royal Salute" - HYDE PARK sy ULSTER   PURE IRISH LINEN   FAST COLOURS

Left: The T-towel is an unapologetic play upon visual and typographic tautology.

Above: On special anniversaries and birthdays Royal Gun Salutes are fired from various London locations. Here the King's Troop Royal Horse Artillery is rendered as fashionably 'mod'. Military uniforms were popular items in the Carnaby Street emporium, I was Lord Kitchener's Valet.

These linen tea towels were designed in six reversible colourways by Juliet Glynn-Smith for Terence Conran's Habitat. Habitat introduced modern style to the British high street and directly into homes with the Habitat catalogue launched in 1969.

This Habitat tea towel is adorned with an engraving from Le Maître D'Hotel Francaise of 1822, a seminal volume by the celebrated chef, Marie-Antoine Carême. Also known as the King of Chefs and the Chef of Kings, Carême worked across most of the courts of Europe.

Left: Rendered in a vibrant contemporary colourway with complex patterning and framed within a dark background, *Birdcage* by Ulster Weavers has the impact of the multi-textured psychedelic poster, pioneered in the USA by graphic artists such as Wes Wilson.

Above left: Rightfully alarmed, a vocal turkey takes fright and fails flight as it scrambles above an exotic recipe for Christmas dinner that includes roasting the bird with pineapple slices and a pint of warm, dark rum.

Above right: Evoking the prevailing interest in the Victorian revival that occurred in the late 1960s, *Pheasant Fantasia* by Ulster Weavers illustrates a typical formal centrepiece found on 19th century dining tables.

Your ship comes in with all you need in the kitchen!
Hard luck, all on the teatowels!
Flowers for the garden
and over the rainbow to love.

Designs by Natalie Gibs
and David Pocknell.

Replete with graphic distillations of high 1960s psychotropic counterculture, this point of sale installation promotes vibrant early work realized by veteran designers Natalie Gibson, Ian Logan and David Pocknell.

Gibson stamps signature heart shapes within fields of abstract forms in bold shades; Pocknell plays punning text against surreal images while Logan frames figurative compositions with the precision of an Oriental rug.

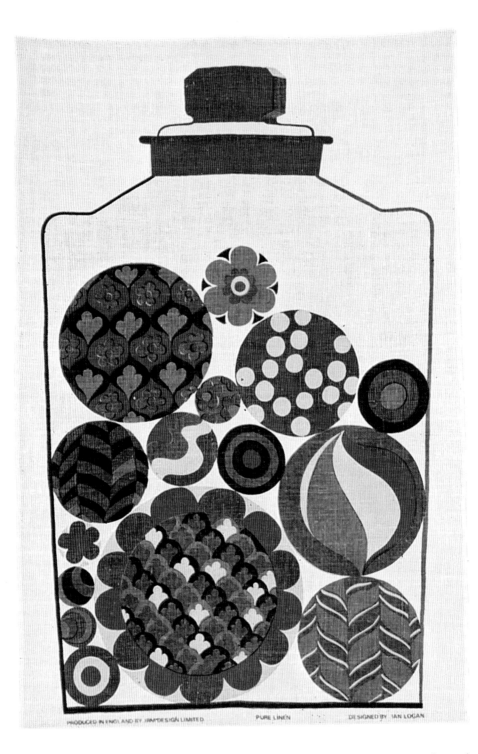

PRODUCED IN ENGLAND BY IRM DESIGN LIMITED   PURE LINEN   DESIGNED BY IAN LOGAN

Designed by Ian Logan, *Candy Jar* features baubles, marbles and bulls eyes, animated by disparate richly hued patterns – swirls, spots, hearts and daisies – contained within a glass-stoppered jar.

In a classic Pop-Art vs. Op-Art 1960s confusion, Ian Logan's *Floribunda* design enhances stylized generic florals with vivid colours and shifting, kaleidoscopic patterns.

With its rich hues and intense patterning of acanthus intertwined with morning glory, this design is redolent of Middle Eastern rugs and suggestive of an aesthetic from the Indian sub-continent, a popular destination on the 'hippie trail'.

In a recollection of the lotus mandala, a transcendental metaphor of heightened spirituality surmounting the material in both Hinduism and Buddhism; this design reflects a prevailing interest in all things Eastern.

Jonelle

The archetypal '60s flower, the daisy, is rendered in flat, graphic form by Pat Albeck for Jonelle, the own-label brand of the John Lewis Partnership, a high-end department store. It was printed by a then John Lewis subsidiary, Stead McAlpin, based in Cummersdale.

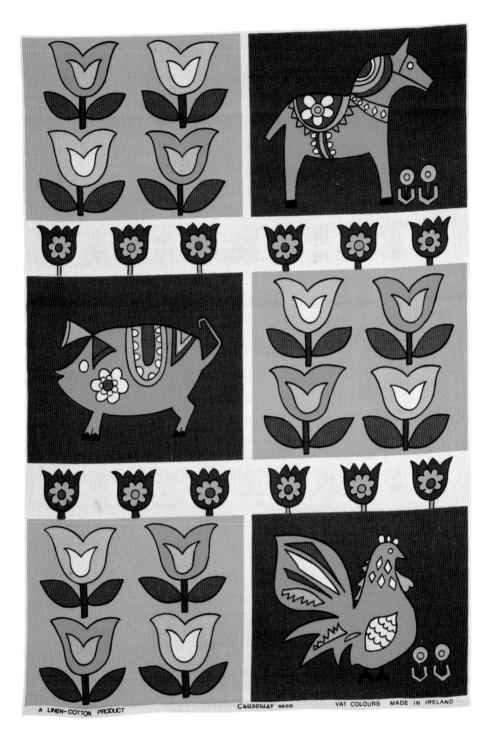

A LINEN-COTTON PRODUCT   CAUSEWAY REGD.   VAT COLOURS   MADE IN IRELAND

The Causeway trademark belonged to Henry's (Belfast) Ltd. and ran from the early '60s until the late '90s. This linen and cotton product asserts that it is printed with vat colours, a process patented by E.I.Du Pont de Nemours & Co in 1952.

THE 1970S

'There was a move towards
graphic design and illustration;
it was very much part of the times —
everyone was designing tea towels.'

IAN LOGAN, GRAPHIC DESIGNER

SEVERAL disparate threads informed the design aesthetic of the 1970s. These shared a commonality by being rooted in the past, from the tightly organized patterns inspired by Owen Jones from his treatise on the decorative arts, *The Grammar of Ornament*, published in 1856, to a continuing interest in an augmented William Morris style, infected with psychedelia. The 1970s kitchen also reflected this upsurge in nostalgia, with the introduction of wholesome, natural materials, such as hand-woven baskets, vintage kitchenalia and antique floral jugs, to the domestic interior. In 1975, during a period active with the second wave of feminism as women aspired to eschew the submissive domestic role, the English writer Shirley Conran published the book *Superwoman*, aimed at busy women, coining the phrase 'Life is too short to stuff a mushroom'. Ironically, women donned dainty floral frills and pinafores as the faux country house 'below stairs' design revivalism intensified.

Any Modernism of the previous decade was largely replaced by a fully fledged desire to return to nature, with images evoking a rural past that only existed in some imaginary golden age. This was typified by Welsh-born designer, Laura Ashley, who popularized small retro florals, drawn from her personal archive of early 19th-century printed cotton fabric samples. The commercial success of her earlier designs, based on Victorian playbills, prompted Ashley to start researching other historical print sources for patterns, and it was with the advent of the 1970s that the label received global recognition for its wholesale homage to the past. In similar vein, Portmeirion Potteries introduced the pastoral overtones of the 'Botanic Garden' range of decorative floral designs by Susan Williams-Ellis, the daughter of architect Sir Clough Williams-Ellis who built the Italianate village of Portmeirion in North Wales. Together with her husband Euan Cooper-Willis, they established the Portmeirion Potteries after they took over two small ceramics concerns, A.E. Gray Ltd and Kirkhams, in the early 1960s. First launched in 1972, 'Botanic Garden' was replete with illustrations adapted from Thomas Green's *Universal Herbal, or Botanical, Medical and Agricultural Dictionary* (1817), and soon became a kitchen staple. A range of non-ceramic accessories, including tea towels, followed.

The Jazz Age, flappers and cocktail shakers were revisited with the resurgence of Art Deco as a trend. This was exemplified by print designer Bernard Nevill at London store Liberty, and by the opening of the fourth and final Biba shop on London's Kensington High Street. This department store offered a cinematic glamour reminiscent of 1930s Hollywood. Everything was designed to be subordinate to the overall look, from fashion and furniture, to tea towels, and even the labels on tins of foodstuffs.

Many of the more successful printed-furnishing companies were convertors rather than manufacturers, taking raw, unprocessed cloth known as greige from the mills, and processing it to a finished commercial product by dyeing, printing or other methods. This was the case with the John Lewis Partnership of which Cavendish Textiles, created in 1930 by Walter H. Halstead, was a subsidiary. It introduced tea towels to its repertoire in 1973.

Illustrator Belinda Lyon first introduced her own brand of psychedelic whimsy in the late 1960s, when Oxfam – the first UK charity to introduce a commercial model to its shops – began to sell own-brand merchandise consisting of the designer's first two tea towels. The elephant and giraffe were initially produced in three colourways and were selected for the London Design Centre – at this time still known as the Council for Industrial Design, prior to the opening of the Design Centre shop in 1971. New designs were added to the range each year, with 20 different animals available in the series by 1979.

This period was particularly fruitful for Pat Albeck as she began her association with conservation organisation The National Trust for Places of Historic Interest or Natural Beauty – or the National Trust as it is more commonly known. In an interview about her career Pat said, 'There were no National Trust shops then, in fact hardly any museum shops existed; it was the beginning of a new style of shopping. I was designing things that people might be tempted to buy at the end of a visit to a National Trust house or garden. This influenced my style. I was using line drawing as my work became more representational and my colour became more muted, to go with the historic houses. Also, it meant that I really had to learn to draw buildings accurately. Many of my designs were for specific properties, which I always visited, so I got to know a lot about the English countryside.'

The tea towel has long been associated with the holiday souvenir, a whimsical purchase, which provides a reminder of the location and is also a cheap and cheerful present for those left behind at home. Overall aesthetic direction was subverted to the designer's need to celebrate local features; a beach front, a funicular railway, a Ferris wheel, an aerial view of the pleasure gardens – very similar in style to the postcards on sale. Tea towels purchased in Scotland, Ireland and Wales inevitably included national emblems – the Scottish thistle, the Welsh daffodil, the Irish shamrock, or even regional recipes such as the Cornish pasty or cawl soup from Wales. These were executed with varying degrees of graphic sophistication.

Originally a small fabric print company producing prints for fashion designers, Ian Logan
formed JRM Design alongside fellow graduates from the Central School of Arts (now Central
St Martins), subsequently producing designs on cushions, tablecloths and tea towels.

Featuring all the accoutrements of the newly fashionable beverage within the portals of a
decorated cupboard, Ian Logan's design *Coffee Cupboard* exudes '60s graphic style overlaid
with the later hippie 'flower power' in contrasting colours produced by vat dyeing.

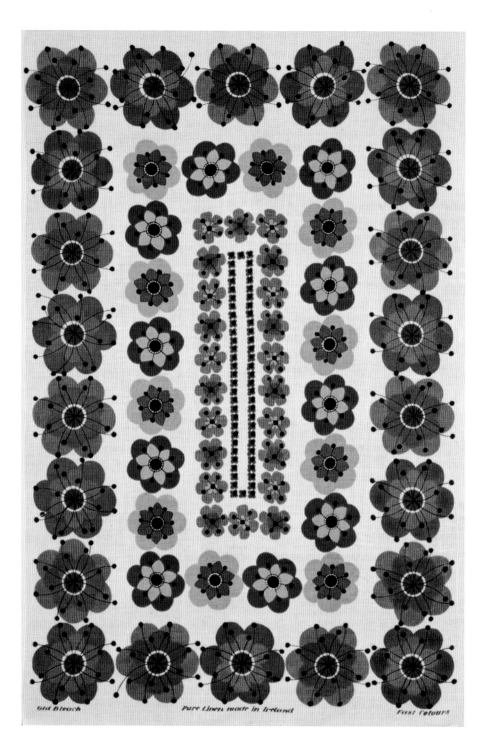

The Old Bleach Linen Company opened in Randalstown in Northern Ireland in 1864. The manufacturer commissioned designs from leading artists such as Marion Dorn, Ashley Havinden and Paul Mansouroff. It was one of the first companies to screen print onto textiles.

A half-drop composition of identifiable garden species, this tea towel reasserts the value of realist clarity. It is as true to the English country garden as a vintage seed catalogue, from campanula to cyclamen and on to bellis, primrose, viola and auricula.

A playful depiction of naïvely drawn creatures to illuminate the biblical story of Noah's Ark in which Noah, his family, and representatives of all the world's animal species are saved from a cataclysmic flood. Designed in full colour by Ulster Weavers.

Dunmoy by Moygashel, a manufacturer of fine linen goods for the aristocracy founded in the 1780's and based in the Northern Irish village of Moygashel in County Tyrone. By the mid-20th century, Moygashel linens were a high-quality brand exported across the world.

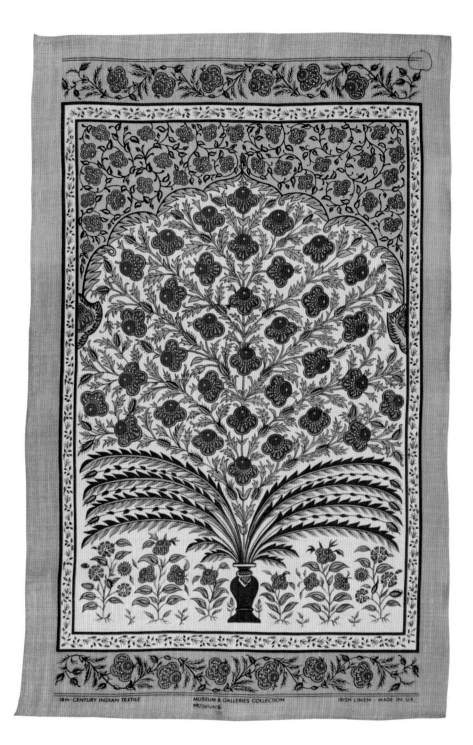

18th-CENTURY INDIAN TEXTILE   MUSEUM & GALLERIES COLLECTION   IRISH LINEN : MADE IN UK
MUSEUMS

A 19th-century multi-patterned Indian textile is the inspiration for Ulster Weaver's Museum and Galleries collection. Below a decorative spandrel, a spray of exotic red flowers fountains from a central vase, replicating an overall architectonic form shared by Hindu temples.

The artwork for a tea towel produced by Ulster Weavers with a theme suggestive of Christmas. The holly, ivy, berried yew and the Christmas rose motifs are worked into an all-over paisley design within a decorative border.

The tea towel commemorating the silver wedding anniversary of Queen Elizabeth II to Prince Philip, the Duke of Edinburgh, follows Ulster Weaver's formal format and traditional colourway of blue and gold. A Celtic-inspired border is interspersed with a white rose.

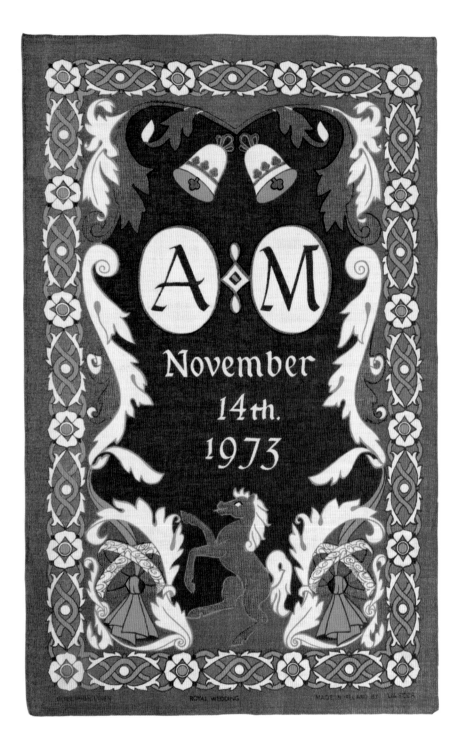

To celebrate the wedding of Her Royal Highness Princess Anne to Captain Mark Phillips, Ulster Weavers followed a similar template to that of the previous design but added, for example, a prancing horse to reflect the couple's equestrian activities.

PÆONIA MOUTAN
Shrubby Peony

Portmeirion's most recognized design is the 'Botanic Garden' range, decorated with a variety of floral illustrations such as this lush peony bloom adapted from Thomas Green's *Universal Herbal, or Botanical, Medical and Agricultural Dictionary* (1817). The range was launched in 1972.

A botanically correct drawing of *Gazania rigens* is framed by the distinctive band of stylized leaves familiar to lovers of the 'Botanic Garden' range of Portmeirion products designed by Susan Williams-Ellis.

CAMEL · A DESIGN FOR OXFAM

Illustrator Belinda Lyon initially worked in advertising before developing her commercial freelance career with illustrations for short stories and books aimed mainly at children and teenagers.

The stylized camel is drawn in typical naïve style enhanced by floral decoration, and is typical of Lyon's clean graphic style that combines '60s Modernism and psychedelic colour contrasts of bright pink and orange with hippie 'flower power'.

Redolent of a faux medievalism, and in keeping with the '70s preoccupation with a Pre-Raphaelite aesthetic, Belinda Lyons 'Great Lovers of the World' series appeared from 1973–1976/77. Subjects included Napoleon and Josephine, Romeo and Juliet, and Antony and Cleopatra.

Notorious outlaw Robin Hood and Maid Marion appear surrounded by an intense arrangement of stylized flora and naïvely expressed fauna redolent of Pisanello's *The Vision of Saint Eustace*. The demeanour of the protagonists conveys an uneasy amalgamation of innocence and dissipation.

Renowned for its innovative advertising, and in a bid to increase its market share by appealing to women, Guinness depicts a woman wearing a dress similar to that featured in John Singer Sargent's *Portrait of Madame X*, while holding a glass of the Irish stout.

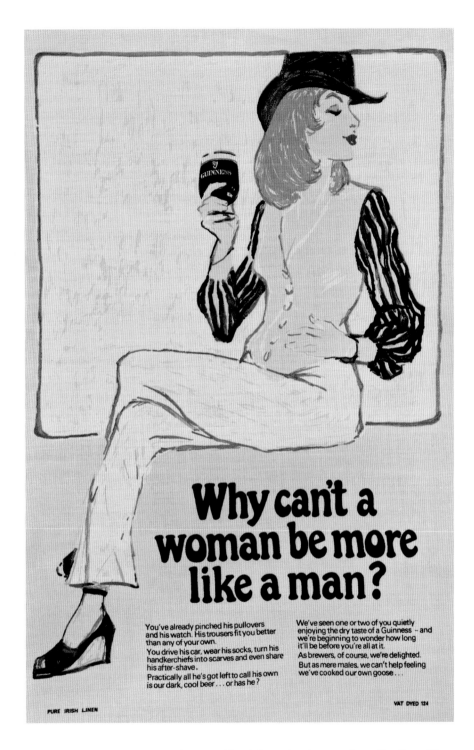

In an era familiar with the second wave of feminism, the slogan – from the film of George Bernard Shaw's play *Pygmalion* – is a rhetorical question implying that women already have it all. The image has the resonance of artists such as Henri de Toulouse-Lautrec.

Elevating the souvenir tea towel to an art form, Pat Albeck deploys architectural drawing with a formal placement of subject matter to create an informative illustration of various Scottish castles held by The National Trust.

Designed by Pat Albeck, this tea towel shows various views of Derbyshire's Hardwick Hall, an architecturally significant Elizabethan country house designed by the architect Robert Smythson for the redoubtable Bess of Hardwick.

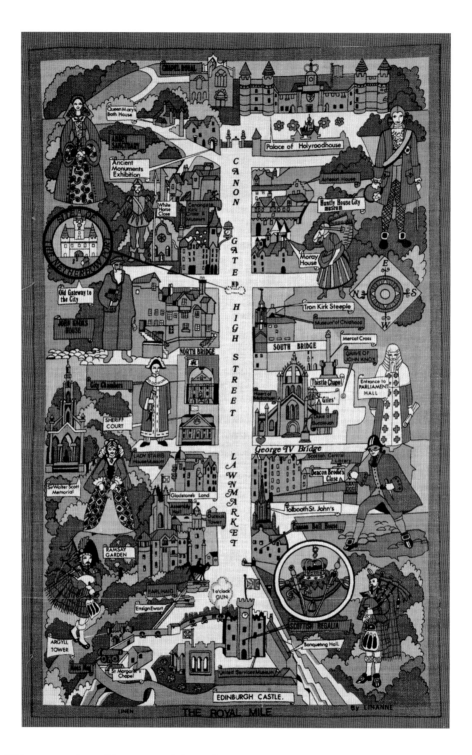

This tea towel provides a map of the main thoroughfare running through Edinburgh, the capital of Scotland. The Royal Mile details significant locations that are pertinent to the history of Scotland – in particular Edinburgh Castle and the Palace of Holyroodhouse.

A crudely executed holiday souvenir of the West Country, this tea towel nevertheless provides a sunny charm, featuring a naïvely described interior of a fisherman's cottage, complete with cat – and the addition of a local recipe.

Seated at a spinning wheel (Wales is renowned for its wool textiles) the woman wears the traditional National costume of Wales – red and black checked betgwn, or bedgown, shawl, white cotton fichu and the unique Welsh hat.

A souvenir tea towel featuring the Jolly Fisherman, a character first seen on a railway poster declaiming 'Skegness is so bracing', drawn by the master of the cheeky seaside postcard, graphic artist Donald McGill (1875–1962).

THE 1980S

'The best shabby chic is not created but an expression of how you are by nature. Natural grace and style helps.'

MIN HOGG, FOUNDING EDITOR OF
***THE WORLD OF INTERIORS* MAGAZINE, 1981**

INCREASINGLY known as the 'designer decade', a newly expanding consumer culture during the 1980s bought into the concept of 'lifestyle' marketing, in which the domestic interior played a major part. It was an era of conspicuous consumption and heralded the emergence of the 'yuppie' – the Young, Upwardly mobile (or Urban) Professionals satirized by American journalist Tom Wolfe in his 1987 novel, *The Bonfire of the Vanities*.

Open-plan kitchens became popular, as walls and doors that traditionally separated distinct functional areas, such as the living room, dining room and kitchen disappeared. It was a concept designed for family living, with the introduction of sofas and rugs and large, all-purpose tables for family dining. Grander, country-house style kitchens, a throwback to the 18th century, became prevalent with bespoke, hand-crafted units. An essential component was the AGA range cooker, particularly with the introduction of the first electric model in 1985, which featured a useful bar across the front from which to hang tea towels. It was an aspirational, aristocratic look that resulted in grandiose designs – large-scale floral bouquets, elaborate gilding and twisted scroll forms on chintz. These appeared in urban kitchens, as well as in country homes. The British company, Warner, under the aegis of designer Eddie Squires, produced the 'Stately Homes' collection, including patterns such as *Marble Hall*. The trompe l'oeil effects of traditional decorative accessories, such as passementerie, appeared in prints including *London Tassels* by Mandy Martin in 1987. Laura Ashley's previous preoccupation with diminutive floral designs evolved into a grander decorative idiom of the country-house look, with large-scale designs and more formal patterns.

The first publication of the influential magazine *Interiors* appeared in November 1981, founded in the UK in London by Kevin Kelly, with Min Hogg as editor. In 1983 the magazine was bought by Condé Nast and it began publishing internationally under the name *The World of Interiors*. The magazine promulgated the new obsession with decoration, paint effects such as faux marble and rag-rolling, swagged curtain pelmets and Roman blinds, which even appeared in the kitchen.

Historic houses and stately homes provided a cornucopia of inspiration; those owned by the National Trust were open to the general public and became a leisure destination throughout the decade. Pat Albeck continued to design, not only tea towels, but also a coordinated range of products, such as table linen, kitchen textiles and ceramics for the National Trust gift shops.

In contrast, at an international level, an urban style of vibrant geometrics was created in 1981 by Italian architect and designer Ettore Sottsass, who founded the design collective Memphis. Named after the Bob Dylan song, 'Stuck Inside of Mobile with the Memphis Blues Again', it was a reaction to the Bauhaus mantra of 'Form follows function', which shunned the purely decorative. Sourcing 1950s kitsch, Art Deco and 1960s pop culture, their unconventional and playful use of primary colours, and uninhibited patterning and texture introduced the notion of Postmodernism to interior design. This theoretical outlook utilised period styles and references, treating the past as one huge antique supermarket. This broke the established rules about style and incorporated the notion that 'anything goes', as pattern provided a transformative role on domestic objects.

Timney Fowler, a partnership forged by artist Sue Timney and graphic designer Graham Fowler in 1980, introduced a Neoclassical collection of bold black-on-white and white-on-black images that proved enormously influential on the domestic interior market. Playfully deconstructing historical motifs in a way that retained all the grandiosity of the original but none of the reverence, the representations of engravings of classical statues and architectural fragments was particularly aligned with the consuming interest in the 'designed interior'.

In contrast to the swags and swathes of the designer-driven kitchen was the popularity of 'shabby chic', a term coined by Min Hogg that encompassed faded chintz, painted furniture worn to expose the timber beneath, simple fabrics such as mattress ticking and pastel linens and painted cabinets. Such informality, evocative of cosy kitchens, well-loved household objects and mismatched china, successfully tapped into a desire for informality – kitchen suppers rather than dinner parties.

Ulster Weavers follow their template for commemorative royal tea towels. Royal occasions – such as weddings – were of considerable commercial significance and resulted in a profusion of ephemera, including tea towels.

A cheerful addition to the Christmas kitchen, designed by Pat Albeck for the National Trust. The cleverly constructed illustration of a Christmas tree is festooned with the prolific gifts from the seasonal song, 'The Twelve Days of Christmas'.

Pat Albeck was inspired by the samplers at Montacute House, a late-Elizabethan mansion in South Somerset for this design for the National Trust. Samplers derive their English name from the French *essamplaire*, loosely meaning 'to be copied'.

Printed on Irish linen and designed for The National Trust by Pat Albeck, *Wax Fruit* acknowledges the prevailing interest in Victoriana. Various species are displayed in a glass dome, a popular decorative device in the 19th century more usually containing specimens of taxidermy.

Created by Ulster Weavers at the time of Bananarama, *Flashdance* and *Jane Fonda's Workout* video, *Flash* presents a dégradée sports stripe on a strong diagonal to create a sense of dynamic movement fit for a yuppie kitchen.

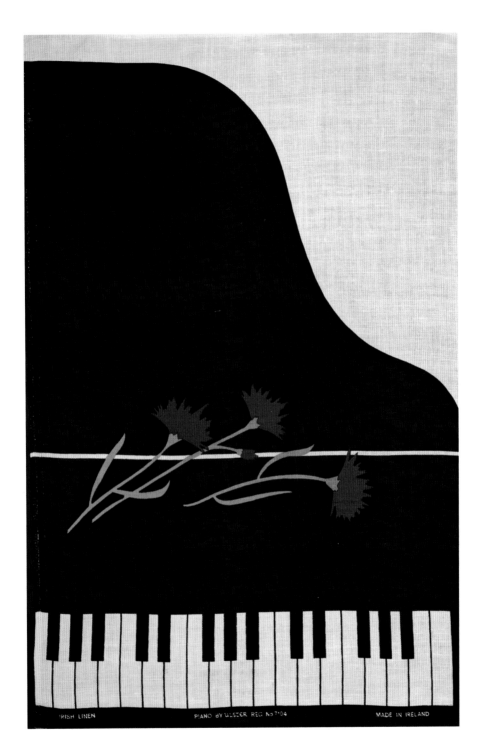

Designed during the cocktail era by Ulster Weavers, the spray of carnations cast over the surface of a glossy grand piano purports to convey the '80s sophistication and decadence conveyed in a Jack Vettriano poster of a piano bar.

THE 1990S

'An old vintage dress fabric inspired
my first ironing-board cover – the
idea proved so popular that many
more vintage-style items, ranging from
tablecloths and seat cushions
to tea towels, followed.'

CATH KIDSTON, DESIGNER AND BUSINESSWOMAN

THE MINIMALIST 1990s was a period when essentials were laid bare, particularly in the kitchen where design reverted to the 1930s ideal of being a laboratory-like space, although for many there was a continuance of the country weekend, 'Sloane Ranger' eclecticism of architectural salvage, early oak and vintage treen. The pared-back ethos was perceived as emblematic of a 1990s urban lifestyle, and timeless but abundant kitchen linens of sober integrity and modesty were now required, perhaps with a faint recollection of Gallic cuisine. Rubber floors, hi-tech appliances (hidden behind doors without handles), and white tiles in a half-drop brick-bond repeat, resulted in the antithesis of the aspirational grandeur of the previous decade, and provided a template for the fashionable kitchen. The vogue for open, loft-style living space and industrial chic produced bare brick walls and polished copper pipes. This pragmatism was furthered by the adoption of rational kitchen linens, emblazoned solely with jacquard text stripes declaiming work functions – 'glass cloth' or 'dish cloth'.

Graphic design became the ruling aesthetic as distinctive packaging provided the only colour amidst the polished concrete, limestone and stainless steel. Exuberant pattern almost disappeared in the modern domestic interior to be replaced by monochrome texture and sophisticated pared-down prints.

The long lines and clear spaces of the minimalist interior were challenged by the notion of 'modern vintage', purveyed by designer and entrepreneur Cath Kidston, who opened her first shop in London's Holland Park in 1993. Offering a compelling and commercially successful version of 'below stairs' rather than the aristocratic 'above stairs' so prevalent in the 1980s, Kidston's aesthetic was one of charming nostalgia for the domestic life of the country house and the kitchen realm of the 1950s housewife. Kidston spearheaded the obsession with vintage style by renovating 'junk' furniture with bright gloss paint, 1950s-inspired polka dots and faded florals, gingham tablecloths and red ricrac braided aprons, providing a comforting and cosy aesthetic for a generation of women who preferred to idealize rather than practise domesticity. One of Kidston's first designs was an ironing-board cover with a distinctive floral print, epitomizing the Cath Kidston look.

Designer and entrepreneur Emma Bridgewater's distinctive spongeware pottery is an evocation of this kinder and cosier interior, one evoking her mother's kitchen, informal and hospitable. She began to make pottery in 1984, having had an epiphany in her search for a pair of cups and saucers for her mother's birthday. As she writes in her memoir, 'I went to one of those old-fashioned china shops there used to be lots of, in search of cosy shapes and colourful patterns … But none of the china bore any relation to the feeling of Mum's kitchen. Every day she mixed old things from markets, or china out of Granny's cupboard, with things bought on holiday abroad, big chipped Deruta mugs, Masons' Brown Quails and plates from Habitat with pink rims.'

English earthenware, particularly Staffordshire, proved the touchstone, and the company Emma Bridgewater formed flourished as she combined traditional ways of crafting pottery with the decorative technique of applying simple patterns with a cut sponge. Subsequently many designs were also adapted for application onto a growing range of other products, including glass, cake tins, picnicware, wallpaper and tea towels.

In 1995 Ulster Weaving Homewares was awarded the Royal Warrant as suppliers of kitchen textiles for Queen Elizabeth II. Based in Holywood, between Bangor and Belfast in Northern Ireland, the Ulster Weaving Company was originally founded in 1880, and throughout the late 19th and early 20th century it continued to spin, weave, bleach and finish the high-quality linen for which Ireland, and Ulster in particular, are famous. The first kitchen textiles appeared in the 1960s, and since then the company has been at the forefront of tea-towel production and design. The company is particularly renowned for tea towels commemorating royal events. As current designer for the company Jennie Harvey says, '… working on something which involves our Royal Family is a tremendous privilege. The commemorative tea towels have to have a classic feel as fans of the Royal Family are quite traditional, but I like to offset this with a contemporary look, as well as injecting some of my own creativity. I go through the archives of work we have done previously for the Royal Family and take inspiration from some of that.'

In 1957 Rena Ames Harding hatched the original flat graphic illustration of a colourful Wellsummer rooster. After several reincarnations, Cornelius Rooster ™, or Corny ™, gained airbrushed 3D realism in the '70s and persisted as tea-towel merchandise into the 1990s.

Though little more than a basic condiment, Oxo has been perennially a stalwart contributor to the revenue streams of advertising agencies. In this promotional tea towel, the palindromic brand name lends itself to a border surrounding an illusory kitchen apron.

Quintessentially Kidston, *Paper Rose* features naturalistic sprays of roses in subtle shades of peach in a half-drop repeat pattern on a grey ground.

This small overall multi-directional print is designed to complement the large-scale
Paper Rose pattern opposite, the tea towels to be sold as a pair.

Ulster Weavers employs an ogee mirror repeat system to accommodate parading gaggles of geese. Constrained within a border of a tumbling daisies are elements found in traditional paisley patterns.

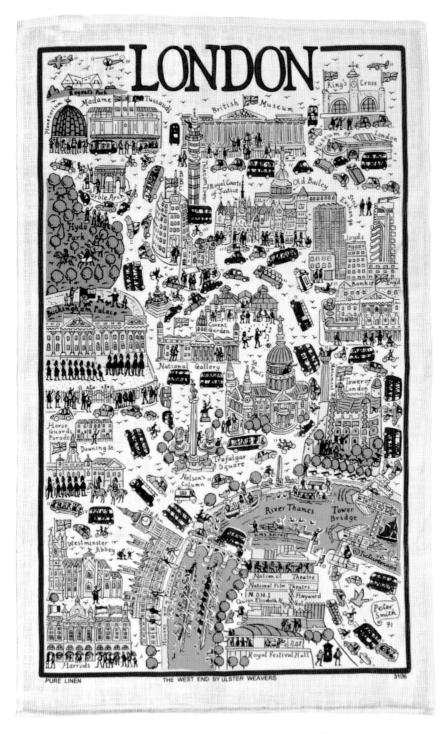

An overview of London's West End by Ulster Weavers. Maps are an obvious choice of purchase, both as a useful guide to the area and as a souvenir of a trip to the capital – or other city.

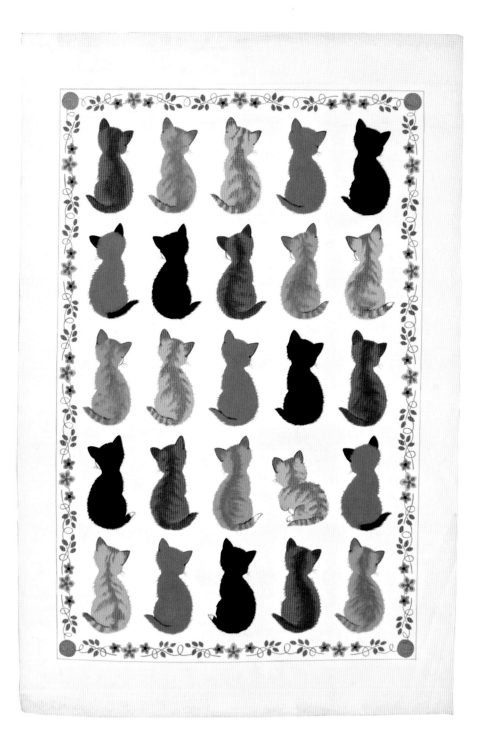

Preparatory artwork for *Kittens* produced by Ulster Weavers. Versions are still in production: *Kittens Arrived* and *Cat's in Waiting*, alongside *Cat's Arrived*. Here, interest is provided by the single crouching kitten.

Ulster Weavers evokes the simplicity of the embroidered sampler in the format of a calendar. Historically, the spot motifs, stylized flowers and border patterns of a sampler would subsequently be put to use in the decoration of clothes and domestic furnishings.

Toast & Marmalade, a signature design by Emma Bridgewater with distinctive font, was first introduced into the textile range in 1994, although this version is from 2013.

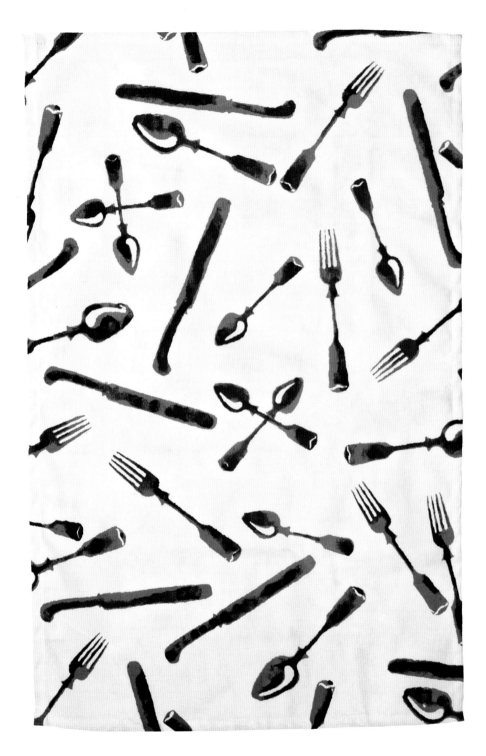

Knives & Forks, from 1995 is a monochrome multi-directional design by Emma Bridgewater featuring carefully placed cutlery. The knives, forks and spoons are allowed to bleed off the edge of the tea towel, creating a free-floating pattern.

BRIDGEWATER BIRDS

Bridgewater Birds from 2004 favours the watercolour depiction of British avian species. With a casual disregard for scale, this twitchers' guide is bereft of text – and consequently enigmatic to all but the plover lover and wagtail watcher.

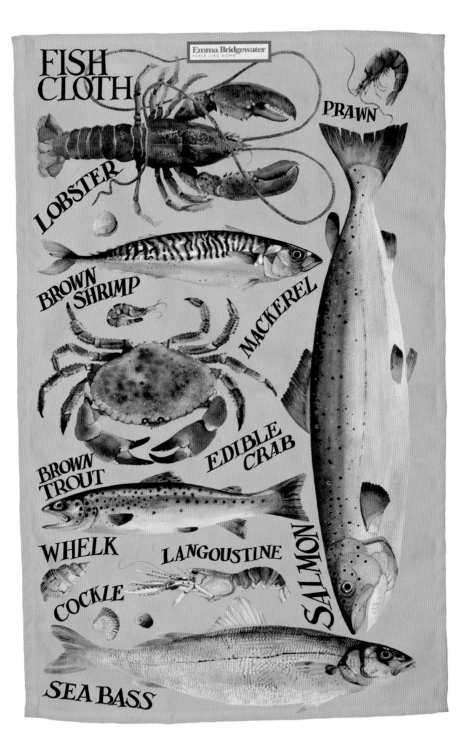

An illustrated tea towel doubling as a shopping guide to culinary fish and seafood, rendered with forensic watercolour detail by Matthew Rice for Emma Bridgewater in 2016.

Designed in 2014, Emma Bridgewater's *Blue Hen & Border* features strong horizontal rows of textured pattern in ribbon repeat, interspersed with marching hens. Blue and white is a perpetual kitchen favourite.

Zinnias (top left) replicates the sponge-ware effect of the matching Bridgewater ceramics, while *Butler's Sinks* (top right) and *Black Lab* (bottom left) deploy the distinctive font. The bold patterns of fashion label Dollyrockers inspired *Hearts and Flowers* (bottom right).

An exercise in nostalgia, an idyllic summer's afternoon is conjured up in *Tea in the Garden* with croquet on the lawn, the duck pond, shady trees beneath a sunny sky, and a table set for tea (with Emma Bridgewater crockery).

For Emma Bridgewater, arranging a patchwork of pottery on a kitchen dresser is a source of delight. Here the tea towel showcases various examples of the designer's informally arranged china.

POSTMILLENNIAL

'[Tea towels are] an old-fashioned form of democratic art … cheap paintings for people who'd never think to – or maybe could never afford to – own an original painting.'

SCOTT KING, GRAPHIC ARTIST

IN THE YEARS since 2000, the perpetual city life vs country living dichotomy came to favour bucolic indulgence over Spartan asceticism. Nest-building flourished in the uncertain years following the financial crash of 2007–8, with the Danish notion of hygge appealing to those whose preferred option was for comfort and cosiness. A renewed enthusiasm for home cooking also rendered the invisible kitchen of the minimalist 1990s obsolete. The trend for concealing everything behind closed doors, white walls and stainless-steel accoutrements was no longer perceived as desirable.

The design of the millennial kitchen was fuelled by an interest in 'vintage', or 'retro' as vintage came to be known. *Festival* (1955) and *Zambesi* (1956) designs by ceramic designer Dorothy Jessie Tait, *Salad Ware* (1956) by Terence Conran for pioneering ceramics company Midwinter, and *Homemaker* by Enid Seeney for Ridgway Potteries, became sought-after collectables. Robin Day's design classic, a polypropylene injection moulded chair with metal legs, designed in 1963 for S. Hille & Co., was popularly used at the kitchen table. Scandi-style, a Scandinavian design movement characterized by simplicity, minimalism and functionality, which first emerged in the 1950s in the five Nordic countries of Finland, Norway, Sweden, Iceland and Denmark, replaced the stainless-steel surfaces and sleek units of 1990s minimalism with form-pressed wood, a neutral colour palette and natural textures.

The trend for what came to be called mid-century modern, a concept that dominated postmillennial design, was heralded in part by the major exhibition staged in 2001 of the work of both Robin and Lucienne Day, further consolidated in 2003 by the exhibition held by the Glasgow School of Art of the work of Lucienne Day. This resulted in the designer's textiles being made available once again under the auspices of 'classic textiles' – digital reprints of Day's original designs. Her *Black Leaf* tea-towel design from 1959 was re-imagined by Habitat in 1999 for use as a duvet cover, and in 2003, in conjunction with London design store twentytwentyone, three of the original tea-towel designs were relaunched, *Too Many Cooks*, *Night and Day* and *Batterie de Cuisine*. London store Heal's also looked to the past with a series of tea towels with images sourced from their archive of posters from the mid-20th century.

This preoccupation with mid-century design is also evident in the aesthetic of Dublin-born designer Orla Kiely, who first established her brand in 1995, producing ready-to-wear collections, homeware, furnishings, luggage and accessories, all emblazoned with her instantly recognizable graphics. Although her tea-towel designs contain elements of the representational, the graphic flatness of the motifs gives a feeling of abstract pattern. The designer's unique colour palette is equally distinctive, with bright colours offset with various tones.

Post-millennium, there is a renewed appetite for royal memorabilia, due in the main to the longevity of the reign of Queen Elizabeth II. Her Golden Jubilee was celebrated in 2002, the Diamond Jubilee in 2012, the Sapphire Jubilee in 2017, and her Majesty's 90th birthday in 2016. The marriages of younger members of the Royal Family has also fuelled a plethora of souvenir tea towels, evidencing a rather more sophisticated aesthetic than that seen in the tea-towel designs of previous decades.

Conversely, tea towels with a radical message can be viewed in the same light as the slogan T-shirt and poster art as an immediate and unavoidable way of communicating a point of view. The Radical Tea Towel Company was founded by the Pearce family in South Wales, prompted by the desire of Beatrice Pearce to find a politically-themed birthday present for a family member. Together with husband Tim and son Luke, the family decided to create a collection of tea towels, with the aim of encouraging left and liberal-minded people to proudly display their political and social beliefs. Quotes from inspiring figures such as Mahatma Gandhi, Martin Luther King Jr., Mary Wollstonecraft and Maya Angelou, together with strong graphic reproductions of activist posters from the era of women's suffrage, make clear the views of the householder.

Angela Harding is one of the most commercially successful designers. A Rutland-based fine-art printmaker, wood engraver and artist, she is an exemplar of a successful relationship between the fine and applied arts. Her tea towels feature British birds and animals, usually inhabiting a definite location and with an atmosphere of place and season. The technique is one in which line is of prime importance. A sheet of linoleum or vinyl is incised with a V-shaped chisel or gouge for the relief surface, with the raised (uncarved) areas representing a reversal (mirror image) of the parts to show printed. The block is then inked with a roller and subsequently impressed onto paper. The actual printing process can be done by hand or with a press. To add colours to the work Harding uses hand-cut paper stencils that are then used with a silk-screen mesh. The combination of water- and oil-based inks gives the work a quality of both softness and clarity, which is then translated onto cloth by the expertise of Suffolk-based printers Stuart Morris.

In this era of the ubiquitous dishwasher, the resilience of the habits and value structures embedded in the discerning accumulation and exhibition of tea towels could well be taken as the faint propitiation of the unacknowledged, but enduring, household deities of stability, sustenance and home.

a life in pattern

25 MAY – 23 SEPTEMBER 2018

FASHION AND TEXTILE MUSEUM

orla kiely

The appeal of pattern lies in its regularity. *A Life in Pattern 1*, designed by Orla Kiely for an exhibition at London's Fashion and Textile Museum, displays horizontal rows of crisply drawn mugs in blocks of colour.

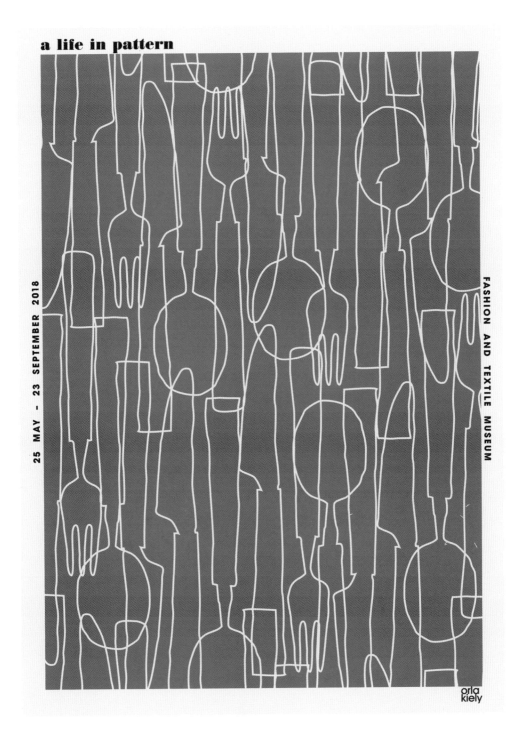

a life in pattern

25 MAY - 23 SEPTEMBER 2018

FASHION AND TEXTILE MUSEUM

orla kiely

A Life in Pattern 2 features ghostly traces of layered cutlery as an all-over
one directional print, reversed out of a khaki background, designed by Orla Kiely.

Recalling the clean, fresh minimal abstraction of form seen in the 1960s, the *Oval Flower* design has a single, central floral motif contained within a variation of the signature stem and leaf pattern familiar to the Orla Kiely label.

With typical clarity of form and distinctive colour palette the graphic distillation of the various motifs – owl, elephant, hen and pear – contain elements of representation even though the overall effect is one of abstraction. Designed by Orla Kiely.

With a history of promoting modern design, particularly under the auspices of Sir Ambrose Heal, Heal's is synonymous with combining good design with industrial production. Taken from a mid-century poster, this tea towel has been updated by in-house designer Charles Feeney.

This tea towel was sourced from a poster advertising 'The Economy with a Difference',
a collection devised to help Heal's survive the 1930s' Great Depression. The range was
marketed towards households with an annual income of £50 or more a year and a telephone.

This was designed by Charles Feeney from a poster commissioned to celebrate the opening of the Heal's exhibition at the Festival of Britain in 1951 – a showcase of art, science and technology that marked the end of austerity following World War II.

A playful evocation of breakfast essentials in a tea towel designed for London store Heal's by renowned London-based artist and illustrator Rose Blake. The design exploits the possibilities of a simple two-colour palette.

Ulster Weavers celebrates the 100th birthday of Queen Elizabeth the Queen Mother. The rose is the national flower of England but also associated with Aphrodite, goddess of love, making it appropriate for one of the most enduringly popular members of the Royal Family.

Jennie Harvey, chief designer at Ulster Weavers, records 'The border is traditional and ornate, and is rich blue with golden tones ... with lots of colours associated with royalty, such as blue, purple and gold all drawn into the template'.

To celebrate the wedding of Catherine Middleton to Prince William, Cath Kidston provides a light-hearted illustration of the bride entering the portals of Westminster Abbey observed by a cheering crowd.

In marked contrast to the formality of earlier examples of celebratory tea towels concerning Royal events, this witty and informal tea towel designed by Cath Kidston for the Queen's Diamond Jubilee features the Queen's favourite breed of dog, the Welsh corgi.

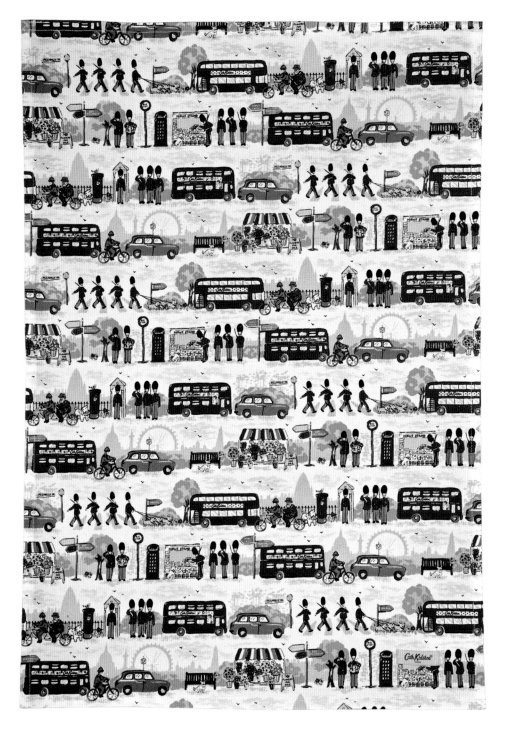

Against a background of London landmarks, Cath Kidston arranges rows of horizontal stripes featuring the iconic Routemaster London bus, interspersed with marching rows of soldiers from the Royal Guards.

London Town by Cath Kidston presents a seductive view of the city featuring well-known landmarks such as Buckingham Palace and Tower Bridge, as well as London's iconic black cab and Routemaster bus, in a half-drop, spot repeat.

The design for the *Mickey and Minnie Bouquet* tea towel marks the global collaboration between Disney and Cath Kidston, with vintage sketches of Minnie Mouse combined with a re-coloured floral print from the Cath Kidston archive, *Spitalfields Rose*.

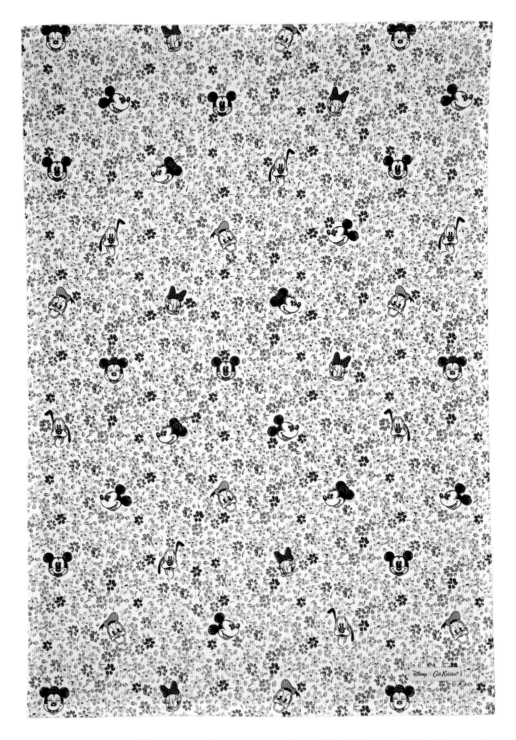

Mickey and Friends Ditsy is a small-scale companion to the *Mickey and Minnie Bouquet* tea-towel design. As with the previous design, the tea towel features Mickey's famous friend before she adopted her iconic polka-dot bow.

Lush Designs

Marie Rodgers and Maria Livings studied painting and printmaking at Maidstone Art College before starting their business Lush Designs, designing and manufacturing homewares. With *Beetroot* they capture the vigour of naïve illustrations in a medieval herbalist's tome.

Lush Designs

Lush Designs' love of colour and characteristic quirky prints continue in this series of tea-towel designs, in which primal carrot hues are asserted in the singular bold motif of their *Carrots* tea towel.

There is an air of allegorical reference in the *Fox and Cubs* tea towel by Lush Designs, as linocut and woodblock prints have frequently been used to illustrate *Aesop's Fables*. The bold decorative rendering of innocent cubs and alert vixen suggests a wider narrative.

Lush Designs

Sprouts from Lush Designs has all the hallmarks of an early horticultural illustration of a specimen plant with underground elements and superstructure retained intact. The print cleverly counterbalances colour infill and linear outline between the two images.

With its *Big Fish* tea towel, Lush Designs alludes to the historic diversity of London's dock architecture of warehouse and wharf. The wider maritime heritage is summoned from the depths by the comic whale shark, snorkeller and coral.

The Tall Ships flotilla assembling at Portsmouth is celebrated in a loose schematic graphic map in this tea towel by Lush Designs. It further suggests the location by recalling HMS Victory of Trafalgar fame, with the Solent sporting a few mythic creatures from the deep.

A design based on a 1911 image by Margaret Morris in the Suffragette colours of purple, green and white produced by the Radical Tea Towel Company. The banner features the initials of The Women's Social and Political Union, the leading militant organization campaigning for Women's suffrage in the United Kingdom from 1903 to 1917.

Deploying classic socialist aesthetic concepts, English artist and illustrator Walter Crane (1845–1915) produced annual cartoons to commemorate May Day, which were reproduced in *Cartoons for the Cause*. *A Garland for May-Day 1895* purports to contrast the beauty of nature with the lives of the factory labourers.

A digitally enhanced section of George Cruikshank's savage cartoon of the Peterloo Massacre, which occurred at St Peter's Field, Manchester, England, on 16 August 1819. Cavalry charged into a crowd that had gathered to demand the reform of parliamentary representation, killing 18 people and wounding over 600.

"When class-robbery is abolished every man will reap the fruits of his labour."

William Morris, 1884

RADICALTEATOWEL.COM

William Morris (1834–1896), an English designer, visionary and social activist founded the Socialist League in 1884. He was associated with the British Arts and Crafts Movement, and the tea towel by the Radical Tea Towel Company features one of his most well known works, *The Strawberry Thief*.

With his dystopian vision, Matty Bovan is one of British fashion's most innovative designers;
the tea towel displays something of a regal self-portrait with the halftone backdrop redolent
of the technique of Pop Artist, Roy Lichtenstein.

Playful mark making dusted with areas of colour feature on this tea towel design, the result of collaboration between fashion label Art School, artist Dominic Myatt and Selfridges.

Utilizing her signature text, and featuring the logo designed by the artist Lucien Freud, Bella Freud makes a simple declamatory statement in a tea towel designed specifically for London store Selfridges.

Under the direction of Charlotte Stockdale and Katie Lyall, the London-based creative partnership Chaos designs luxury tech and lifestyle accessories, including this tea towel, for the Selfridges pop-up shop.

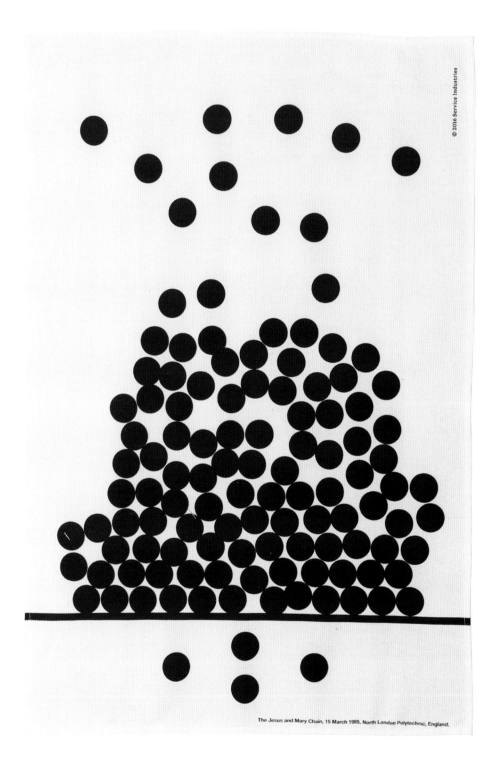

Event-based artwork by graphic designer Scott King from King's product shop Services Industries. In reductive form, the tea towel marks the North London Polytechnic gig of Scottish post-punk rock band The Jesus and Mary Chain. Screen print on cotton, 70 x 50cm (27½ x 19½in), 2016.

King perceives the tea towel as ripe for subversion, creating a set dedicated to the press communiqués of The Angry Brigade – the left wing revolutionary group from the 1970s. *This Is Not The Jet Age*, felt-tip pen on cotton, 70 x 50cm (27½ x 19½in), 2016.

Above: Angela Harding's lithograph, *Blackbird and Rose Nest*, translates readily to usage as a tea-towel print. Generally her prints used in this way have a softly rounded perimeter which functions largely in the same manner as a photographic vignette, encouraging the eye to focus on the core subject matter.

Right: *Bringing Back the Tree* exploits the graphic clarity afforded by the harsh contrasts and buffered stillness of a snowscape. In Harding's adept composition of foreground intimacy and background distance, even the prancing lurcher and striding figure are perceived as still and peaceful.

Left: Derived from a print originally commissioned by *Country Living Magazine* in 2016, this tea-towel design – *Seal Song* – depicts the seal colony and blustery foreshore of Bardsey Island off the North Wales coast. Created in a process combining colour linocut and screen print, Harding embraces the British inter-war print heritage of naturalist landscapes, nurtured by the Grosvenor and Heathersley Art Schools.

Above: *Look Out* combines linocut and screenprint to position the dark graphic forms and toned colour bands respectively. In a clever exploitation of the colour precept of depth perception created by placing pale imagery to suggest foreground and darker tones to imply distance, the covert lookouts are disguised in the immediate foreground by the shared, fragmented rendering of foliage, fur and flora.

Angela Harding's *Shooting Stars* tea towel was originally a colour lithograph, providing the opportunity for varied textures, such as the stippled star field and the loose cross-hatching and tonal rendering of the awestruck hare in the dramatic moon-shadowed foreground.

Harding's *Stopping by the Woods* is the product of both linocut and silk screen processes. Dark printed areas give depth to the horizon and beyond, while the wily fox in the foreground undergrowth has more delicate tones.

BIBLIOGRAPHY

FURTHER SOURCES

Albeck, Pat, *Printed Textiles* (Oxford University Press, London, New York, Toronto, 1969).

Bridgewater, Emma, *Toast & Marmalade: Stories from a Kitchen Dresser, a Memoir* (Saltyard Books, 2014)

Casey, Andrew, *Lucienne Day* (Antique Collectors Club, 2014)

Hine, Thomas, *Populuxe* (Bloomsbury Publishing Ltd, London, 1988)

Jackson, Lesley, *Robin & Lucienne Day: Pioneers of Modern Design* (Princeton Architectural Press, New York, 2001)

Kidston, Cath, *Vintage Style: New Approach to Home Decorating* (Ebury Press, 1999)

Konig, Rita, *Rita's Culinary Trickery* (Ebury Press, 2004)

Sparke, Penny, *As Long as It's Pink: The Sexual Politics of Taste* (Pandora, San Francisco, California, 1995)

York, Peter, *Modern Times: Everybody Wants Everything* (William Heinemann Ltd. London, Melbourne, Toronto, Johannesburg, Auckland, 1984)

Angela Harding https://angelaharding.co.uk

Bella Freud www.bellafreud.com

Cath Kidston www.cathkidston.com

Chaos www.chaos.club

Dominic Myatt https://dominicmyatt.com

Emma Bridgewater www.emmabridgewater.co.uk

FSG Design www.fsgdesign.co.uk

Rose Blake www.iamroseblake.com

Ian Logan www.ian-logan.co.uk

Laura Ashley www.lauraashley.com

Lu Jeffery www.lujeffery.co.uk

Lush Designs www.lushlampshades.co.uk

Windett Design www.windettdesign.com

Matty Bovan www.mattybovan.com

Orla Kiely www.orlakiely.com

The Radical Tea Towel Company
   www.radicalteatowel.co.uk

Scott King www.scottking.co.uk

Service Industries www.serviceindustries.co.uk

Stuart Morris https://stuartmorris.co.uk

Ulster Weavers www.ulsterweavers.com

INDEX

ACKNOWLEDGEMENTS

With thanks to Kristy Richardson at Pavilion Books. Particular thanks to
Allan Hutchings, for his marvellous photography as ever, and to Anna Keane
at Heals, Angela Harding, Chris Large of fsg design, Dominic Myatt, Hannah
Crewe at Liz Matthews P. R., Ian Logan, Imogen Hunt and Rebecca Rodgerson
at Laura Ashley, Jennie Harvey at Ulster Weavers, Jeremy Parrett special
collections archivist Manchester Metropolitan University, Leigh Willot and
Tom Phillips at Emma Bridgewater, Lisa Patten at Bella Freud, Lu Jeffery, Luke
Pearce at The Radical Tea Towel Company, M. Faye Prior collections facilitator
York Museums Trust, Maria Livings of Lush designs, Mandi Lennard, Matty
Bovan, Natasha Ryder and Xenia Xenophontos at Cath Kidston, Paula Day
and Wilhelmina Baldwin at the The Robin and Lucienne Day Foundation,
Rose Blake, Scott King and Stuart Morris.

Digital restorations by John Angus, University of Derby.

PICTURE CREDITS